# Parenting with Grace

●

Practical & Spiritual Strategies
to Raising Godly Seed

●

**Sadé Tate**

Copyright © 2022 by **Sadé Tate** All rights reserved Published by beyondthebookmedia.com All rights reserved. No part of this publication may be reproduced, distributed, or transmitted in any form or by any means, including photocopying, recording, or other electronic or mechanical methods, without the prior written permission of the publisher, except in the case of brief quotations embodied in critical reviews and certain other noncommercial uses permitted by copyright law. For permission requests, write to the publisher, addressed "Attention: Permissions Coordinator," at the address below. Limit of Liability/Disclaimer of Warranty: While the publisher and author have used their best efforts in preparing this book, they make no representations of warranties with respect to the accuracy or completeness of the contents of this book and specifically disclaim any implied warranties or merchantability or fitness for a particular purpose. No warranty may be created or extended by sales representatives or written sales materials. The advice and strategies contained herein may not be suitable for your situation, You should consult with a professional where appropriate. Neither the publisher nor author shall be liable for damages arising here from. Beyond The Book Media, LLC Alpharetta. GA www.beyondthebookmedia.com The publisher is not responsible for websites that are not owned by the publisher. **ISBN –978-1-953788-69-6 (Printed)**

# Acknowledgement

I want to thank my natural and spiritual parents for instilling in me what it means to parent with grace.

I want to thank Latisha Moore and Vanessa Frazier for your encouragement and support as well as assisting with editing this book.

# Table of Contents

| | |
|---|---:|
| Acknowledgement | 3 |
| Introduction | 7 |
| Chapter 1: It Starts With You | 11 |
| Chapter 2: Getting Whole | 17 |
| Chapter 3: It Takes a Village | 25 |
| Chapter 4: Shaping & Molding Young Minds | 37 |
| Chapter 5: Managing Emotions | 43 |
| Chapter 6: The Power of Confessions | 49 |
| Chapter 7: My Seed is Not the Enemy | 57 |
| Final Thoughts | 67 |
| Reference | 69 |
| Author Bio | 71 |

# Introduction

There is a multitude of information that exists about parenting. Many people describe it as a hard job; however, parenting is more than a job you clock in and out of on a daily basis. It's a forever calling. Whether this calling came unexpectedly or was planned, it's clear that you, as a parent, guardian, or grandparent, need the grace of God to raise your child(ren), which I will also refer to as your seed.

With any seed, you are to provide the proper environment and nutrients for it to grow properly. The same care and diligence happens with Godly parenting– nurturing and raising your seed in the admonition of the Lord (Ephesians 6:4), so they can fully grow into what God has called them to be. If you do not tap into God's parenting grace and rely merely on your intellect and abilities, you will constantly be worried, stressed, and frustrated. Settle in your soul that God did not leave you alone to raise your seed. If He blessed you with them, He has made provision for you to raise them. All you have to do is tap into His grace.

To tap into this grace, you first need to accept and acknowledge the triune God — God the Father, God the Son, and God the Holy Spirit. God the Father knew you would be a parent before you did. He knows all your proclivities, quirks, hurts, pains, and insecurities. Nothing is a surprise to God. Everything you need to parent can be found in the Word of God.

Parenting is a "spiritual work" that will require a growing walk with the Father, Son, and the Holy Spirit. Most people read books, listen to podcasts, and watch videos without going to the One who created your seed and download wisdom from the Holy Spirit. Trial and error aren't your greatest teachers. Instead, you should seek guidance from the ultimate teacher. There is nothing wrong with seeking help; however, you should first seek help from the triune God.

Deciding to parent in your own strength will disrupt your peace and cause you to miss the joy and beauty of this parenting season. Why would you forego, avoid, and dismiss God when it comes to parenting? There could be many reasons. Were you absent from a godly role model? Have you been disappointed by God? Did you even think to fully entrust your seed to Him? Trust that He knows what's best and will never leave you nor forsake you (Deuteronomy 31:6) as you raise your seed.

*Parenting with Grace* will highlight the spirituality and practicality of parenting. It will bring light to common misconceptions about raising your seed as well as highlight ways you can tap into the grace of God as you parent your child(ren). As you read this book and go on this journey, there will be areas that you will find that you are doing well and other areas you have to modify. If you are doing more things wrong than right, know that God sees you and will reveal to you what you need to know to start from where you are in order to parent with grace.

# Chapter 1:
# It Starts With You

In a hedonistic society where our needs, wants, and desires are most important, we rarely take the time to do a self-inventory. When you're having problems with your seed, it's common to look at what they are doing wrong. Parents seldom humble themselves and reflect on their parenting practices. Many people think parenting starts with evaluating your child, but it starts with you. To parent with grace, it's essential that parents consistently commune with God and allow the Holy Spirit to reveal things in them that may negatively affect their seed. Introspection needs to take place to ensure that unresolved issues such as fear, guilt, shame, rejection, and bitterness are not causing an unhealthy relationship with your seed. God is the ultimate healer and can help you, but you must first identify these areas as problems.

It's important that you seek to parent from wholeness, not brokenness. Your unresolved issues can negatively affect your interactions with your seed and cause you to be too strict/overprotective or too permissive/aloof in your parenting. The Holy Spirit can help you find that "sweet spot" of parenting and what your child may need during certain seasons of their life.

There are times when the Holy Spirit will strategically lead you to be stricter than usual or perhaps allow you to give your child a little more freedom, but this is more about what's beneficial for your seed than trying to overcompensate for the damaged areas in your life. For example, guilt and shame can lead to feelings of condemnation and unworthiness. This could be a result of past mistakes you have made in your parenting (i.e., blaming yourself for your child getting hurt because you weren't watching them or excessively disciplining that causes physical and emotional harm to your seed) or perhaps an unhealthy lifestyle you lived or are living (i.e., drug/alcohol abuser, promiscuous, excessive workaholic, etc.).

The shame of not being able to consistently provide food or adequate housing can impact your parenting skills. Some parents can always seek to make their children happy and always give them what they want. While you shouldn't seek to intentionally make your seed's life miserable, you should not always give in to their demands. Children may bring up your mistakes or make you feel guilty about missing one of their games or performances; however, that should not merely cause you to buy them things to cover your mistakes or compensate for you not being present. In addition, reflect on whether you're buying them things only because you are overcompensating for not having material possessions growing up.

Be mindful of feelings of rejection and bitterness that can make you harsh and uncompassionate. If unresolved, these emotions can harden your heart. It can lead you to always over-talking your seed and never listening to them. It also can cause you to be too strict. Whatever causes rejection or bitterness (i.e., someone leaving you, not feeling accepted, past abuse, etc.), pursue wholeness and allow God to heal these broken areas of your life.

Reflection Questions:

1. What areas of brokenness do you have that need to be repaired by the Holy Spirit?

2. What current or past parenting mistakes do you need to forgive yourself for making?

3. What lifestyle changes do you need to make to become the parent God calls you to be?

# Reflections

# Reflections

# Chapter 2:

# Getting Whole

In the previous chapter, I talked about not parenting from a place of brokenness because these feelings will ultimately spill over into your parenting practices. If you continue to struggle with persistent shame, guilt, rejection, and bitterness, you may need to seek help to get and stay whole physically, mentally, and emotionally. These areas of brokenness can cause you to feel anxious, depressed, angry, and unworthy. The enemy wants you to stay broken and wants you to engage in unproductive ways of parenting your child(ren). Do not be prideful and seek help if needed.

First, you confess to God, seek godly help, and repent over these damaged areas. In that confession/repentance combination, He will show you the roadmap to getting and staying whole. A daily and consistent prayer life is an essential strategy to defeat these negative emotions. Praying is a form of communication with God where you make your requests known, are silent before Him, and give Him room to speak to us. Often, we do all the speaking and do not leave room to listen to His instructions. If your daily plate is full, incorporate prayer into your daily activities. For example, washing dishes even if you have a dishwasher. Folding clothes is another strategic time to pray. Take the dog for a walk or use your commute to work to talk to God. At every light, practice listening for God's quiet voice. Praise and worship are also vehicles for your healing. It's hard to stay in a negative space when praising and worshiping God. Include times of prayer, praise, and worship in your daily life.

Once you've identified where you need help and have confessed and repented over these broken areas to God, He may instruct you to seek help from other resources, such as your church, mental health professionals, and friends. Do not let feelings of shame or embarrassment keep you from seeking help. Depending on your deep-rooted negative emotions, you may need to seek help from all three.

Your church can be a resource. Consistently staying under the Word of God by opening the Bible, attending church services, and bible studies are maintenance strategies to keep your peace and stay whole; however, churches may also offer support from small groups depending on the areas you need support. In addition, you can all seek help from your pastor or the church's leadership team. That said, finding a church where you and your children can find fellowship is important. Your church is a source of prayer and support as you go along your journey of wholeness.

Mental health professionals are also another resource you can take advantage of on your journey to wholeness and powerful parenting practices. Please note that you do not have to choose between getting support from your church or mental health professionals. You can seek support from one or the other or both. God has His people everywhere, so take the time to ask if the mental health professional is a Christian. There's often a negative stigma with seeking help from mental health professionals, but God created his men and women of God to be equipped with spiritual gifts. Godly counsel versus counsel from a worldview is extremely different, so choose well. Counseling is not only for people with mental health diagnoses such as anxiety, depression, bipolar disorder, etc. This can be one of the vehicles God uses for your healing. You may see a mental health professional for a couple of sessions or possibly longer, but the length is determined by the issues you need to process and work through. Again, do not just choose anyone; seek God for wisdom about who to choose.

Your friends can also be a great source of support for you. Now, these are not just any friends and should not be confused with acquaintances. These are people you can open up to and are safe for you to express your feelings. In the words of Dr. Marcia Bailey, they can be your "battle buddy" and "accountability partner" who will listen or give you sound advice. They will also pray for and check in on you. They should be honest and trustworthy individuals who won't share your conversations with others. These friends can also be a source of accountability to ensure you don't slip back into negative patterns or thoughts. You may find these traits in one person or a couple of people, but be prayerful and be led by the Holy Spirit in your decision.

Taking steps to get whole and break the chains holding you hostage will lead you to be a healthier person mentally and emotionally and lead to you being the parent God has called you to be. This is a bold step that the enemy does not want you to take. Instead, he will have you stay broken and in a posture of defeat. If negative feelings or emotions arise as you seek help, push past them. On the other side, there will be victory and wholeness that will benefit you and your family.

Reflection Questions:

1. Do I need to seek help from other individuals, groups, or professionals? If so, ask God what your next step is to seek help.
2. Are there any Godly battle buddies and accountability partners God is calling you to connect with? If so, list their names.

# Reflections

# Reflections

# Reflections

# Chapter 3:

# It Takes a Village

You may be familiar with the phrase "it takes a village" when referencing raising children, insinuating that you will have to seek help during your parenting journey. To parent with grace, you must seek help and wisdom from the Holy Spirit. The Holy Spirit is your helper and will lead and guide you on how to raise your seed. He will reveal to you who will be a part of your village. Even if your village is small, there is a point where you will have to ask for help; however, with the help of the Holy Spirit, you will have wisdom when choosing who to entrust your seed.

Your school and child care provider is part of your village. This may seem like a stretch, but guess what? If you work outside the home, your child spends most of his or her time with a teacher and child care worker. Therefore, you need to pray and seek God about where they should attend school and continually cover your child's teacher, school, and daycare provider in prayer.

Spiritual attacks come against schools, school personnel, and child care facilities, so it's important that once you decide where your child should attend school, you continue to lift them in prayer each day, especially the staff interacting with your seed daily. After all, they now have an influential position in your child's life, so you do not make this decision without seeking God.

Every year your child attends school, make sure you pray that your child gets in the God-ordained classes and that whoever is hired is divinely appointed to that institution. If your child's teacher is indifferent to your moral beliefs, pray that your child will have a divinely orchestrated influence on the teacher. As your child is trained in the way of Jesus Christ, prepare him or her to be prepared to face unbelievers in a godly fashion. Pray for the safety of the environment and the students that your child will come into contact with. Declare a hedge of protection from physical, mental, and sexual abuse.

Remember that your seed's school/child care provider is not your enemy. You shouldn't have a "me versus them" mentality. From personal experience, most teachers/child care providers genuinely care about children. Yes, some work in the profession for the wrong reasons, but that's the minority. Education and child care, especially in this day and age, is not easy. Partner with them to get to know your seed and build a plan to help your seed excel. It's okay to bring up items of concern if they come up but seek wisdom from the Holy Spirit about how to approach these things and don't address them when you're angry.

It's important that you don't jump to conclusions even if you had a terrible experience with a previous teacher or child care provider. Start each year fresh; don't bring old baggage into a new year. You can learn from previous experiences but can't assume that what happened in the past will happen with this new teacher/child care provider. It's easier said than done, but it provides grace for mistakes. You are not a perfect parent, and I am sure you have made some mistakes. For situations that appear detrimental to your seed and there seems to be no peaceful reconciliation, seek God about what to do and whether to change schools/child care providers or possibly switch to home/virtual school.

Consider which family member and or friends should be a part of your village. Do not let your guard down because you've known someone a long time or they are related to you. God knows the innermost secrets of each person and knows which ones will take the important responsibility of assisting you in caring, praying for, and raising your seed. Taking into account how your family and friends raise their children and steward their lives is a good first step in deciding which ones you'll have to be part of your village. However, God knows everyone's heart and knows which ones should be responsible for caring for your child. If the Holy Spirit does not allow you to choose someone to care for your seed, this does not mean they are corrupt or have some deep dark secrets. In this season, particular family and friends have what is needed to impart what your child needs for their purpose and destiny.

As a reminder, be careful who you allow into your child's life. You shouldn't entrust someone with your child ONLY (out of convenience) because you are in a bind and need someone to watch them. Children are very impressionable, especially at an early age. It's your responsibility to protect them. The damages that may happen from someone you know or think you know influencing and putting ideas in their minds or letting them be around people who may harm them by not watching them closely outweigh the benefits. They may meet a need for you now, but more things may have to be cast out because of this connection later.

Be watchful of who you let your kids play and be with- even if they seem okay on the outside and maybe a relative or a family friend. Follow the peace of God. If something does not seem right, take a different course of action, even if you don't fully understand the details.

In psychology, professional counselors see countless scenarios of physical, sexual, and emotional abuse by other children, friends, and family members. Even siblings, parents, and significant others have been identified as abusers. If the circumstances or surroundings don't seem right, take action. You don't have to know all the details to remove your child from a potentially harmful situation.

God knows the beginning from the end and wants your child to be safe and protected. Parents should also consider whether a mental health professional should be added to their village. We discussed in the previous chapter that this might be needed for parents, but there are some children and families as a whole that would benefit from participating in counseling. When this is a step you are considering, it's important that you choose a mental health professional that aligns with your beliefs. Just because they identify with the Christian faith does not mean they share your views on certain topics that may be important to you. Before choosing a mental health professional, you may want to assess your beliefs about certain hot topics and seek to find out where your potential mental health professional stands before allowing them access to your seed. A list of things to consider is below.

1. What are their views on legalized marijuana?
2. What are their views on gender identity and same-sex marriages?
3. If you are a believer that believes in the Holy Spirit with the evidence of speaking in tongues, determine if this is a quality you'd like the counselor to have.
4. What are your deal breakers (i.e., things you won't compromise on)?
5. Do they have to subscribe to a particular belief system or denomination?

If these counselors will be working with your seed, who are especially impressionable, it's important that you know who they are. You don't have to accept a therapist because of their title, role, or degree. You can be respectful and ask questions that are important to you. You rather do your due diligence on the front end than have to change counselors later.

Be led by the peace of the Holy Spirit when choosing a therapist. If you don't have a therapist that aligns with your beliefs near where you live, you can also search to see if there is one outside of your local area that offers virtual services. Once you decide to work with a therapist, give it time to work. You don't get into thought patterns overnight.

Keep in mind that therapy is not magic. You have to do the work. You get out of it what you put in. While it's important to give time to work, also be cognizant of when you need to change. This is not an easy decision; however, at times, it's necessary. With the help of the Holy Spirit, you can choose another one.

Be open and honest with your therapist. If you have concerns, tell them instead of storing up feelings of resentment, anger, and frustration that can be projected onto other family members and individuals around you. The right therapist will help provide clarity and help you think through things. It will give you fresh eyes on your situation.

They will help you see yourself and expose anything you are doing that's contributing to or exacerbating your child's behavior. Sometimes when you're too close to a situation, it's hard to be objective, and you cannot see what you're doing wrong.

Youth ministry is a valuable resource that can benefit families and come alongside and partner with you to raise your seed. Youth workers/pastors pray and intercede on your child's behalf and your family. Some children go to youth workers instead of parents, who can give sound advice. The youth ministry may not meet every day but make sure they go when they have it. It shouldn't be a choice. They will learn and get messages on their level.

Youth ministries aren't perfect, but they seek to be experts, relate to children, and specialize in youth. If your church doesn't have a youth ministry, ask church leadership about it. Even if they can't pay someone full-time on staff, they may have someone who can volunteer in this area. It's important that youth have the opportunity and space with other youth where they can get the Word on their level. Your seed is going through a lot, and they need to be able to rightly divide the Word amongst peers and youth workers. Some things won't come out in the whole group setting or near their parents in the main church. They also may not be as transparent when they have issues with parents, but sound youth workers can help them navigate these challenges with parents, school, siblings, peers, mental health issues, self-esteem, etc.

There is an important place for youth ministry. Effective ones fellowship and teach your children. It's also important that you don't hold youth ministry as a reward and not let them go if they get in trouble because they like going. God can do things in youth ministry He doesn't do anywhere else. I've seen students get clarity on their lives, navigate identity and self-esteem issues, and mend relationships with parents. It's especially important that you see it as a partnership and resource. If they have a parent group, join that as well. Take advantage of all opportunities because you may get hooked up with parents who are going through or who have been through the same things you are going through. It also provides much-needed support and connection.

Don't parent alone. The devil will isolate you and make you think you're a bad parent, but you're not. Take advantage of the support you have and press into God. He has all the answers you need. Surrender to Him and seek His face, and your seed will grow in the destiny and purpose God has for them. There may be some bumps and bruises along the way, but God will work it out for your good. He knows what He's doing.

To parent with grace, you need the proper village around your seed. God has a group of individuals who he has assigned to be a part of your village. He also has a group of friends for your seed that will be iron sharpening friends. Pray over your child's current/future friendships and future spouse early. Make this into your confessions for your seed. Be sure to stay on the offensive and do not let the enemy catch you off guard.

Reflection Questions:
1. Who do I need to add to my village?
2. Who do I need to remove from my village?

# Reflections

# Reflections

# Chapter 4:
# Shaping & Molding Young Minds

The age range of birth to 8 years of age "build(s) a foundation for future health and life success" even though the brain continues to grow and develop through adulthood (Robinson et al., 2017). What does this mean for parents? This means that the early years are extremely important. Parents must instill in their seed who they are in Christ and model Godly living. Build up your seed's self-esteem by reading and showing them what the Word of God says about them before the world can tell them differently.

Allow what the Word says to fill their hearts and minds. Your seed's first introduction to God should be through you. You should model what a person sold out for Christ looks like. This does not mean perfection. It's actually healthy for your seed to see you make mistakes, correct them, and apologize if necessary. This models realistic expectations so that they do not put too much pressure on themselves to be perfect.

At an early age, your seed should be exposed to prayer and know its importance in the life of a Christian. They should also see you pray. As soon as they can speak, you can model prayer for them until they can pray independently. Teach them that prayer doesn't have to be formalized; it's simply talking with God. Children should also see you serving and helping others in and outside the church. Giving back to others and allowing compassion for humanity helps them not be selfish or self-centered.

Make sure you live a life you want your child to emulate. The notion of "do what I say and not as I do" doesn't work with children. They shouldn't see you live a life opposite of what you're trying to teach. For example, you want them to tell the truth and operate with integrity, but they see you lie and scheme. Even if it's something you perceive as a "little white lie," this can confuse their schema and sense of right and wrong when you say one thing but do another, especially during the early formative years. You may have unknowingly modeled some of the negative behaviors you may see in your seed.

Think about what behaviors you've displayed that don't line up with the Word of God. If you need to set up a family meeting, talk about these things and how things will be different moving forward. This will hold you and everyone accountable. Open and honest conversations are needed amongst families. After all, you all are doing life together, and through life, there are ups and downs, and people make mistakes.

It's important to lay the foundation for "uncomfortable or challenging" conversations with your seed early. As much as possible, set the standard for certain topics such as purity and identity before your seed transitions to daycare or grade school. This is because they may interact with peers and adults in these domains that expose them to topics from a secular perspective. Of course, age-appropriate language should be used, which will set the foundation for talks about sex, identity, etc. Often many parents have these conversations too late, and they have to be reactive instead of proactive. Seek wisdom from the Holy Spirit about the correct time and how to present these topics. You can't do these things by the flesh, but you must be led by the Holy Spirit.

Reflection Questions:

1. Are there conversations that I have been avoiding having with my seed? If so, what are those topics, and when should I start having these conversations?
2. Are there any Godly behaviors, such as prayer and worshiping God, that I need to be more intentional about modeling in front of my seed? If so, what are they?

# Reflections

# Reflections

# Chapter 5:
# Managing Emotions

Getting upset or angry is a normal feeling that all adults should know how to appropriately express. However, this is not always the case. When children get upset, it can escalate quickly when not given their desires. This can happen when they do not have the language to express their feelings or the necessary coping skills to manage their emotions. Regardless of why they behave that way, this can cause parents to feel embarrassed and helpless, especially when they are in public. In most circumstances, it's not the proper approach to always cave in to their demands just because they are disruptive.

At times, you have to teach them to manage their emotions and help them understand that they will not always get their way. If they don't learn this at home, the world will teach them, which is not what you want. Using the word "no" teaches them how to deal with not getting their way as adults. Have you ever seen adults have temper tantrums? As a child, many probably got their way and are not used to being told no. They never learned the coping skills necessary to handle things not going their way. This is an essential skill not only for adults but for children. If you find yourself always wanting to give your seed their way, you need to ask the Holy Spirit why this is. You may want to reread the chapters entitled "It Starts With You" and "Getting Whole" because this could be an indication of a deeper issue.

Additionally, children need nonjudgmental, supportive parents. You want your seed to be able to come to you. Nonjudgmental doesn't mean that you don't hold them accountable and can't correct them. Try to remain calm when they tell you things that make you angry, frustrated, or upset. The goal is for them to keep coming to you. You can be honest with them, but do not overreact. This is easier said than done. Just know that the more you drive a wedge between you and your seed because of your reactions, the more they will turn to someone else, and you don't know if that person will give them sound, biblical advice.

As parents, it is essential that we set boundaries and rules. As your seed shows maturity and responsibility, you can let them have more freedom and opportunities. Seek God about what responsibilities you can entrust them with for each season. For example, a smartphone is not a necessity, and most children cannot handle the responsibility of this; it can do more harm than good. Social media is not a must. Just because most children may have access to a service or item does not mean it's right for your seed. As a parent, do not feel pressured into allowing your child(ren) to have things or go places ONLY because other children have access to it.

Children exhibit a range of emotions for various reasons. If your child is always upset, angry, sad, or frustrated, take a step back and ask the Holy Ghost what your seed is trying to tell you. Is there something going on at school? Have certain changes occurred recently in the family? Ask the Holy Spirit and do an analysis. Do not accept "I'm fine" as an answer if you can sense that something is wrong. It may take time to discover the full aspect of what's going on with your seed. This will take time, patience, persistence, and intentionality. Don't quit even if it seems like you're not making progress and you seem to hit a wall. Seek God for wisdom on your next step and what to do next.

Reflection Questions:

1. Am I modeling or teaching appropriate social skills? If not, do I need to seek support or additional training to assist with this? List any areas you need to seek additional support in.

2. Does your child feel safe coming to talk to you? Do they view you as nonjudgmental? Why or why not? If not, what can you do in your realm of influences to change this?

3. What responsibilities can I entrust my child with this season?

4. What things may I need to remove, limit, or place parameters around?

# Reflections

# Reflections

# Chapter 6:

# The Power of Confessions

What are confessions? Confessions are decrees and declarations you are believing God to manifest. They can be written, or you can verbally record them. I would suggest that you have a visual representation of your confessions, whether that's pictures or words. These are reminders of what you are believing in God for. I can remember times writing out confessions with tears flowing down my face. Sometimes I or my family seemed so far from the mark; however, it's important to write them down even if you can't fully see how they will come to pass. The "how" is God's job, not ours. You have to confess what God says, not how you feel.

Your confessions must be biblically based. You don't want to confess something that doesn't line up with the Word of God. Seek God about these confessions. Parents may need to get educated on certain topics to know how to strategically pray and what confessions to write. Verbally say them with your mouth. Don't just think about them. Life and death are in the power of the tongue. (Proverbs 18:21). Therefore, you want to speak life to those things you want to grow and manifest in your life, such as your child having the mind of Christ and operating in the obedience of the Lord and that the Holy Spirit leads them. Even if these things haven't physically manifested in the earthly realm, still decree and declare your expectations for your seed.

Confessions are important because they release angels who are fighting on your seed's behalf. It's a vehicle God uses to facilitate getting your prayers from the heavenly to the earthly realm. Remember that these things may not happen overnight, especially if there's a lot of spiritual warfare in that area due to the mandate your seed has on their life.

Confessions also help change your mindset and what you believe in your heart. While you may not fully believe or initially see how they will come to pass, your faith will continue to grow as you vocalize these confessions. "With the faith of a mustard seed, you can move mountains." (Matthew 17:20). As you continue to declare them, you will start to fully believe in your heart what you are confessing will come to pass. You continue to say them until you see them manifest. Ask God to overcome any unbelief you have. Some confessions take hours, days, months, years, or decades to manifest depending on the level of warfare assigned to that particular area, but you don't change them based on your current circumstances.

When you first pray, reinforcements are dispatched, and angels are on the move. However, demonic forces can hold them up, as in Daniel 10:13. This scripture depicts the spiritual battle happening in the heavenly realms. Confessions also show and track God's answered prayers. You can update, add, or remove certain confessions you've seen manifested as you read your confession. There are certain confessions the Holy Spirit will have you leave just because He knows the devil will attack your child in that area in the future. Therefore, that area needs to be continually covered even if it looks like your seed is currently having victory and success in that area.

Confessions allow you to also be proactive instead of reactive. The Holy Spirit might show you things and areas the devil may try to attack your seed in the future. You can target these areas in prayer and put them on your daily confession list. It allows you to pray and confess from a place of victory before the devil tries to intervene in this area.

The enemy will try to attack your mind so that what you believe will not come to pass. You have to guard against bitterness and not let it consume your heart. Proverbs 13:12 says, "Hope deferred makes the heart sick." This can be subtle at first and can slowly creep into your heart, so make sure you bind this daily. It can come out as cynicism, jokes, or negative thoughts. You have to take your thoughts captive. You have to take your thoughts/feelings to God if you begin to feel this way. God understands you (Hebrews 4:15); therefore, you can be honest before Him.

As negative thoughts enter your mind, take note of them, cast them out and bind them by confessing. For example, if you are having thoughts about your seed not doing well in school, you may want to confess, "My seed has the tongue of the learned (Isaiah 50:4) and the mind of Christ (1 Corinthians 2:16). My seed will excel in school and have access to all resources to be successful." Think of a negative confession/thought that keeps entering your mind about your child. Next, combat that thought with a positive confession.

Reflection Questions:

1. Do you have daily confessions for my seed? Write down what you need to add and/or remove from your confessions?
2. Are there any delays in prayer that are causing bitterness or anger in my heart? If so, write these down and submit these to God.

# Reflections

# Reflections

# Reflections

# Chapter 7:

# My Seed is Not the Enemy

Say this with me, "My seed is not the enemy." When going through a difficult season with your seed, it can often feel like they are the enemy. You probably spend most of your time and energy trying to reason with them and get them to understand what they need to do or how they should act instead of fighting with your spiritual weapons. The devil would love nothing more than to drive a wedge between you and your seed. If the enemy can turn you against them, he can cause havoc.

I have had countless parents in my office tell me they "give up." I am the first one to say that parenting is not easy, but if you don't fight for your seed, who will? Through the tough times, you must seek help, assistance, community, and ultimately wisdom from the Holy Spirit when you feel like checking out or giving up. Parents often feel this way because they are putting all their energy into fighting the people they see in front of them instead of the enemy they cannot see. Parents should engage in spiritual warfare for their seed.

Ephesians 6 describes spiritual warfare and tells us who the real enemy is. It describes what to do and helps us to develop a battle plan. The devil is not going to let your seed go easily. Depending on the assignment on their life, you may have to target certain areas in prayer more than others. For example, let's say your seed is to be a Rhodes Scholar and develop a cure for a disease thought to be incurable. The devil might attack your child in their mind to think they are not smart and might describe themselves as "dumb." You can combat their negative confessions with your positive confessions in prayer. You should also model for your seed how to do this as well.

Generational curses are things that repeatedly develop in your family line that are meant to hold your family back from their God-given purpose. These are repeated cycles and strongholds for your family. For example, let's say you know that your great grandfather struggled with mental illness, as well as your grandmother and several of her siblings. You see this trend as well in some of your aunts and uncles and your parents. You also struggle with this. It's safe to say that your family line is dealing with a generational curse of mental illness. When you know this, you can eradicate it from your seed, future generations, and bloodline by binding it.

The devil would love nothing more than your seed to struggle with the same thing as all your ancestors and other relatives. Now that the enemy's plan is exposed, what are you going to do about it? You can continue to fight and argue with your seed or fight the real enemy. Ephesians 6:12

says, "For we are not fighting against human beings but against the wicked forces in the heavenly world, the rules, authorities, and cosmic powers of this dark age."

The life of a supernatural parent is one of fasting, praying, decreeing and declaring, loosing, and binding. The TPT version of Ephesians 6:10-11 says, "Now my beloved ones, I have saved these most important truths for last: Be supernaturally infused with strength through your life-union with the Lord Jesus. Stand victorious with the force of his explosive power flowing in and through you. Put on God's complete set of armor provided for us so that you will be protected as you fight against the evil strategies of the accuser!" Here is a description of how you can be strong in the Lord. You have to draw your strength from Him as you battle for your seed. You are instructed to "put on" the armor which means it's a choice. You can try to war your way, but God's way guarantees victory.

What is the armor, you might ask? The armor is found in Ephesians 6:14-19. Metaphorically speaking, the various armor pieces represent truth, righteousness, peace, faith, salvation, and the Word of God. Now you can apply these scriptures to any area of your life the enemy is attacking. For the purpose of this book, we are going to apply them to parenting. I encourage you to read through the chapter independently, but I will briefly provide an overview.

Truth is an important aspect of parenting. The devil often tries to distort the truth and get you to believe His lies about yourselves, your seed, and your family. These lies do not line up with the Word of God. Positive confessions, which were discussed earlier, combat the lies of the enemy. These lies are meant to cause you discouragement as a parent and thwart your seed's purpose and destiny. The lies about yourself that can come upon you are that you don't have what it takes to parent your seed. When you can draw strength from the Word of God, then you can say, "I can do all things through Christ that strengthens me"(Philippians 4:13), including parenting your seed.

God "perfects those things that concern you."(Psalm 138:3). Because you care about your seed, God surely does. Let's believe the truth found in God's Word versus the lies of the enemy. You can't go into battle thinking you are going to lose. You won't be able to fight with vigor and will give up. When thinking about quitting and giving up on your seed, think about the enemy's lies and write positive confessions based on the Word of God to combat these lies. Think about what's at stake; your child's life hangs in the balance.

The next piece of armor you need to put on is righteousness which is right standing with God. The Lord sent His son to die for your sins, but many parents let shame, condemnation, and guilt get in the way of your relationship with Him. You aren't going to fight well if you believe the person you are praying to for help is mad, upset, or hates you. God so loved you and us that He sent His son to die for us (John 3:16), knowing that you would make mistakes and wouldn't measure up, which is why everyone needs Him.

There is no condemnation that can separate us from the love of God (Romans 8:1). It's important to confess to God what you did wrong, repent, and turn away from this mindset or action. All will be forgiven. As a parent, you will make mistakes, but don't let this affect your relationship with the one who loves you and who will give you a strategy to defeat the enemy in the life of your seed.

Your next armor is peace. Peace is a state of calmness and tranquility. Peace and worry can't coexist. This is an area where the enemy often attacks parents. He has them in a constant state of anxiousness and worry to the point where it's accepted as normal. If you are in this state, you aren't thinking clearly or at an optimum level, and the devil can slip in and attack your seed because you didn't see it coming. When has worry led to anything good happening in your life? If you are worried about an area, that's an area you do not fully trust God in. Turn these areas over to God.

Faith is confidence in God that His Word is true. "Without faith, it's impossible to please God" (Hebrews 11:6 ) (NKJV). Put another way, Hebrews 11:1 (TPT) says,

"Now faith brings our hopes into reality and becomes the foundation needed to acquire the things we long for. It's all the evidence required to prove what is still unseen." Do you genuinely believe what you decree and declare about your child will come to pass? If it's hard or difficult at times to believe because of what you are seeing with your natural eyes, ask God to help you overcome any unbelief. If the devil takes your faith, he has direct access to your seed.

Do what you have to do to remain in a posture of faith, from surrounding yourself with faith friends or studying what the Word of God says about faith. When you're vulnerable, be careful what you listen to, what you watch, and who you surround yourself with. Faith quenches the fiery darts of the devil, which are his lies. In your heart, you have to believe that no matter what comes against you, your seed, or your family, no weapon formed against them will prosper (Isaiah 54:17). Quench these attackers with the Word of God.

The Word of God is another piece of armor. Parents need to clothe themselves and their families with the Word. They need to study and know it so they can decipher what is a lie and what is the truth. It's the ultimate manual of parenting.

Meditating on the Word of God exposes, sifts, analyzes, and judges the heart's very own thoughts and purposes according to Hebrews 4:12 (MSG). Proverbs 4:23 (NLT) tells us to guard our hearts above all else, for it determines the course of our lives. The Word sheds light and exposes things in your hearts that don't align with God's Word. The more you saturate yourselves with the Word, the more your families will mirror Christ.

The final piece of armor is salvation. All Christians have knowledge that they have been delivered and saved from the damaging effects of sin. Often, you need to be reminded of this. As parents, you still need the blood of Jesus to repent when you do something wrong. God still loves you despite your mistakes. Jesus wiped your slate clean. Parents also need to do this for their children. Don't hold their past mistakes against them to the point that you can't see the new thing God is doing in them now. Be a model of forgiveness and unconditional love to your seed even if they are in a season of "working on their testimony."

Reflection Questions:
1. Am I treating my seed as the enemy? If so, how can I change my parenting tactics to fight the real enemy?
2. What areas do I need to renew my mind in when it comes to battling for my seed?
3. What are some areas concerning my seed that I need to fully surrender to God?

# Reflections

# Reflections

# Final Thoughts

You have the grace of God to parent during this season. You can choose to parent in your own strength or fully and totally surrender your seed to God. The stakes are high, and if you decide to quit, you leave your seed for the enemy to have his way. If God blessed you with your seed, you are equipped with the tools to raise them in the admonition of the Lord. Keep the mind of a student so that the Holy Spirit can teach you what you need to know about raising your seed. Change your view of how you see yourself. God sees you as fearfully and wonderfully made (Psalm 139:14). The devil is hoping you give up, but you have what it takes. You declare you have what it takes, declare God's promises for your seed, and you will receive manifestation in due season.

# Reference

- Robinson, L. R., Bitsko, R. H., Thompson, R. A., Dworkin, P. H., McCabe, M. A., Peacock, G., & Thorpe, P. G. (2017, July 28). CDC Grand Rounds: Addressing Health Disparities in Early Childhood. MMWR. Morbidity and Mortality Weekly Report, 66(29), 769–772. https://doi.org/10.15585/mmwr.mm6629a1

# Author Bio

Sadé Tate is a writer, speaker, and school psychologist. She earned a B.A. in Psychology from Clemson University, an M.S. in Counseling and Human Systems, and a Specialist Degree in Education from Florida State University. She enjoys volunteering and giving back to her community.

Sadé has actively served youth and their families since 2009. She currently serves in ministry at her local church and serves as a school psychologist, where she consults and provides support for parents, students, and teachers. She is passionate about prayer, connecting families with resources in the community, and teaching parents how to advocate for their children.

www.ingramcontent.com/pod-product-compliance
Lightning Source LLC
Chambersburg PA
CBHW051707090426
42736CB00013B/2585